The Oddsocktopus

Written by
Christian Foley

Illustrated by
Rob Turner

The octopus

who

?

is bored of being an octopus
just looking at rocks

I want to be the first

octopus

wearing...

odd socks!

It's true...

I'm bored of being an Octopus

just looking at rocks

I want to be the first Octopus

wearing...

A necklace
made
from
a
clock!

Knock Knock!!

Who's there?

The **octopus!**

The octopus who

It's true...

I'm bored of being an

octopus

just looking at rocks

with a necklace clock

I want to be the first

octopus

to...

Knock Knock!!

Who's there?

The

octopus!

The octopus
whooooooooooo

The octopus oddsocktopus
clocktopus
flocktopus
how do you doooooooo?

It's true...

I'm bored of being an octopus

just looking at rocks

wearing a necklace clock

friends with a flamingo flock

I want to be the first

octopus

to...

buy the finest binoculars in stock

then tie them to a frock!

Knock
Knock!!

Who's
there?

The
octopus!

The
octopus whooo

oo oo

ooo

oo ?

The octopus oddsocktopus clocktopus flocktopus wok-stock-frocktopus

how do you doooooooooo?

It's true...

I'm bored of being an **octopus**

just looking at rocks

wearing a necklace clock

friends with a flamingo flock

frying broccoli in a wok

with binoculars and a frock

I want to be the first **octopus** to...

show a **shark** a short sharp shock
then run amok feeding choc by the block

to a croc in a smock
in a loch by the dock!

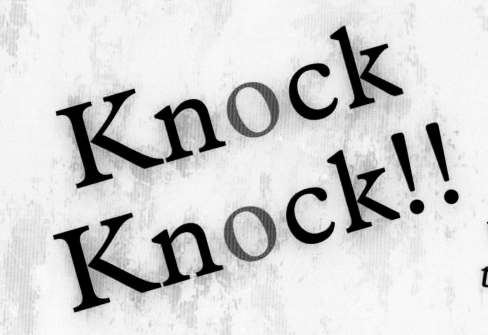

Knock Knock!!

Who's there?

The octopus!

The octopus who

The octopus oddsocktopus clocktopus flocktopus wok-stock-frocktopus shock-amok-choc-block-smock-loch-docktopus

how do you doooooo?

What I've got is the SEA!

A magical shallow reef
moonlight dances in the deep

there are curling swirling trees
with twirling whirling leaves

the turtles and turbots

my tentacles tease

I tend to attend them
with ten tickles

each!

I laugh with glee

I swim with ease

I live as I please... I fit in a squeeze

with all that I need

Knock Knock!!

Who's there?

The octopus!

The octopus who

oooo

ooo?

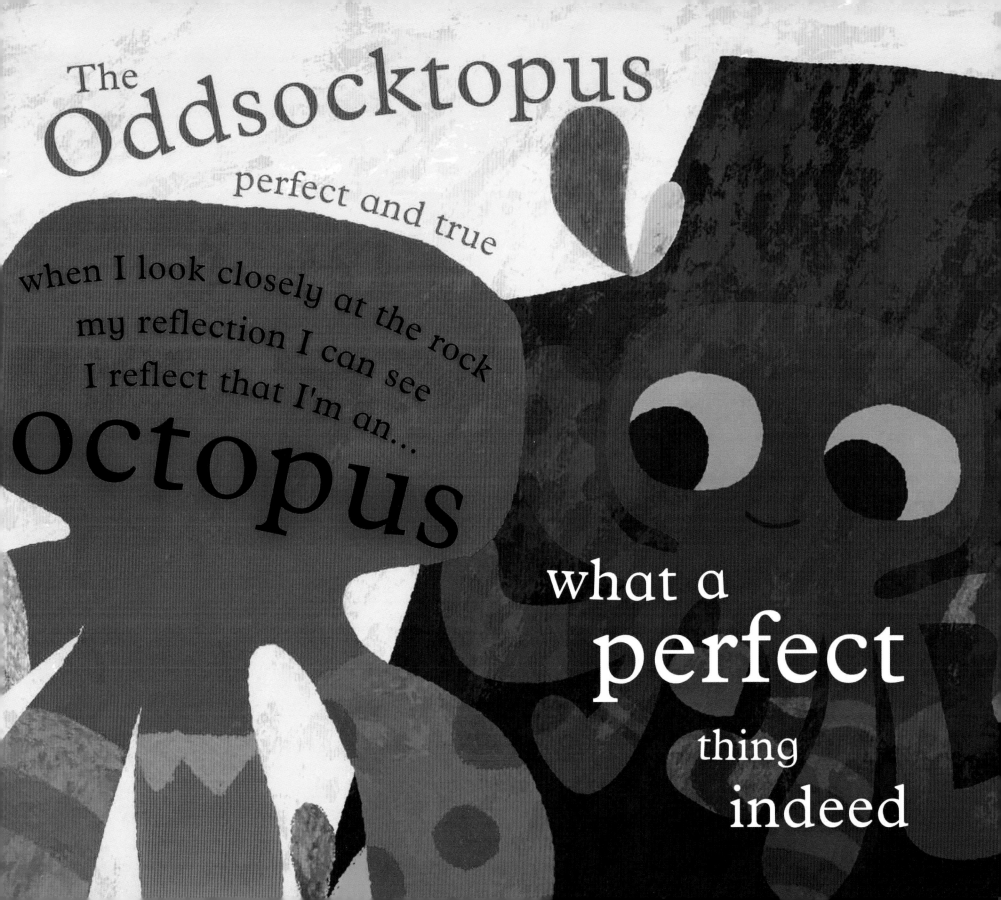

The **Oddsocktopus** perfect and true

when I look closely at the rock
my reflection I can see
I reflect that I'm an...

octopus

what a **perfect** thing indeed

as I **knock** around the sea

it's myself I need to be

I am The Oddsocktopus

and I'm perfect being **me!**